Getting the Mail

For Ann
— 2021

poems by

Cathy Cultice Lentes

Cathy Cultice Lentes

Finishing Line Press
Georgetown, Kentucky

Getting the Mail

Copyright © 2016 by Cathy Cultice Lentes
ISBN 978-1-944899-61-5 First Edition
All rights reserved under International and Pan-American Copyright Conventions.
No part of this book may be reproduced in any manner whatsoever without written permission from the publisher, except in the case of brief quotations embodied in critical articles and reviews.

ACKNOWLEDGMENTS

Grateful acknowledgement is made to the editors of the following publications in which these works, or earlier versions of them, first appeared:

Appalachian Heritage: "Appalachian Wine"
Blueline: "Driven," " Life Work," "Marjolane," "Walnuts"
Cantilever: "Ten Years"
The Comstock Review: "Getting the Mail"
Follow the Thread: "The Slowest Boy in the World"
Now & Then: "Approaching Chester, Ohio," "Passing Poems"
Ohio Connections: "All the Little Schools"
Pine Mountain Sand & Gravel: "Allan," "A Longing Like Noah's," "Drinking Tea at a McDonald's Overlooking the Ohio River at Pomeroy, Ohio," " Farm Bureau Annual Dinner," Fossil Fueled," "Throwing Stones," " Upon Hearing James Still Read 'Those I Want in Heaven with Me Should There Be Such a Place'"
Riverwind: "Heavenly," "Washing the Poem," "Weather Report," "When Wishes Were Horses"
"Approaching Chester, Ohio," was the winner of the year 2000 Appalachian Poetry Competition sponsored by *Now & Then* Magazine and The Center for Appalachian Studies and Services. The poem also appeared in the anthology, *I Have My Own Song For It: Modern Poems of Ohio* (The University of Akron Press), and *Northern Ohio Live Magazine*.
"Fossil Fueled" appeared in the anthology *Quarried: Three Decades of Pine Mountain Sand & Gravel*.

Publisher: Leah Maines

Editor: Christen Kincaid

Cover Art: Sally Stanton

Author Photo: Bartee Photography

Cover Design: Elizabeth Maines

Printed in the USA on acid-free paper.
Order online: www.finishinglinepress.com
also available on amazon.com

Author inquiries and mail orders:
Finishing Line Press
P. O. Box 1626
Georgetown, Kentucky 40324
U. S. A.

Table of Contents

Washing the Poem ... 1
Life Work ... 2
Approaching Chester, Ohio ... 3
Ten Years ... 4
Marjolane ... 5
Farm Bureau Annual Dinner ... 6
Remembering Selma, Ohio ... 7
Upon Hearing James Still Read "Those I Want In Heaven With Me Should There Be Such A Place" ... 8
Allan ... 9
The Slowest Boy in the World ... 10
All the Little Schools ... 11
Throwing Stones ... 12
Fossil Fueled ... 13
A Longing Like Noah's ... 14
Drinking Tea at a McDonald's Overlooking the Ohio River At Pomeroy, Ohio ... 15
A Normal Day ... 16
Passing Poems ... 17
The Road Marked Poetry ... 18
Appalachian Wine ... 19
Walnuts ... 20
Writing the Storm ... 21
Driven ... 22
Weather Report ... 23
When Wishes Were Horses ... 24
Heavenly ... 25
Getting the Mail ... 26

*For my family and friends
of hill and mountain,
river and woods*

WASHING THE POEM

I will never have clean windows.
I haul the necessary water, gather
rags and vinegar, lemon juice
to shine. I climb the ladder
and begin washing winter
from the glass, muddy thoughts,
slow grime. I round the house
but then the garden calls, or clouds,
daffodils burst in early light.
The dog fetches an enormous
stick—one toss—she flies.

Soon the day cools, but
words warm on the stones.
I long for the sheen
of a clean page. I dry
my hands, reroll my sleeves,
for the real work to be done.

LIFE WORK

He wonders what she does each day—
his time compressed by crises,
meetings here, hearings there.
He forgets to eat until he's home,
his sudden hunger stirred
by the sight of her arranging
supper in her way.

He imagines her hours stretched
moment to moment, changing
diapers, scrubbing floors, the dirty
work of marriage. She lives in
slow motion, filing images of
childhood, seasons he will
never know.

He senses there is more to her,
secrets deep in denim pockets,
mysteries put up in Mason jars.
How else to explain the geography
        of her desk,
strewn with glacial mounds of quartz,
forests of fragrant pine, russet leaves,
poems nesting in curved hollows
        of down.

APPROACHING CHESTER, OHIO

Last night the sky ignited.
November trees blazed up
match-struck by the setting sun.
High on the hill, the old courthouse
windows flamed, then flickered
as if lit by candle glow.
Time curled back—
Suddenly horses' hooves
clattered on hardened ground,
cold wheels creaked on stone.
Longing for home,
I pulled my shawl close—
though I had no shawl or house there—
and leaned into my husband's body,
my children's breath rising behind me,
radiant, white as bone.

TEN YEARS

Ten years this house stood vacant.
The woods never forgave us
for trying to take it back.
Birds insist the porch is theirs, nest
after nest, egg after egg. Uneven
floorboards sink toward soil, rotting
slowly back to earth.
Maple trees spread arms to block
our view of cars and people passing by
so even we forget to which world we belong.

Long ago we lost our fear of spiders,
bats, and other creatures that creep and claw.
We painted all the walls forest green, and it
is hard to tell where inside ends and outside
starts. Soon all semblance of civility will
be gone—
we'll fail to dress, eat only what
presents itself, live hairy and howling
under a roof of stars.

MARJOLANE

owns the flower shop, and everyone knows
she can coax life from a hundred-year-old seed.

Her house, aging and ramshackle, but her yard
slows your drive, a masterpiece of odd abandon

like those Christmas displays seen on TV
featuring the world's largest light-up reindeer.

Unlike Eve, she's happy in the garden, preferring green
peace to the tart carnal knowledge of the beasts.

She's pruned two deadwood husbands, choosing
thyme and dirt to be hers alone.

Her children grow like sturdy weeds, unkempt, thorny,
spreading wherever the wind blows

yet rooted firmly in their mother's rich soil, they
never transplant completely.

FARM BUREAU ANNUAL DINNER

Mid-October, all the politicians and faithful are here,
brochures of their promises crowding our meals.
Elbow to elbow, we chew baked steak, speakers
come and go to polite laughter, loud applause.
When the Elvis impersonator steps to the floor,
gold lamé jacket dazzling under fluorescent light,
I know I'm not in Cleveland anymore.
He sings the standards, though he skips
the bump and grind. The crowd, mostly elderly,
endures—they are kind.

Brilliantly, he takes a gospel turn—
By and by, Lord; How Great Thou Art—
I tumble back to childhood, my grandmother
resting in her favorite chair as Elvis swoons
his praise on the stereo, her face, the face
of a woman in love.
No sadness, no sorrow,
No trouble I see—
Her farmhouse couch covered in plastic,
mail-order dishes and fancy flatware
saved for an occasion that never came to be—
There will be peace in the valley for me.

REMEMBERING SELMA, OHIO

Black coffee and ice-flecked milk,
wheat toast spooned with sweet jam,
fried eggs speckled with pepper and salt,
thick slices of sizzling ham,
Pap's mince pie slathered
with breakfast gravy.

Mounds of potatoes, garden dug;
pungent, vinegary greens;
Grams' macaroni and cheese
erupting chunks of un-melted cheddar;
Uncle Slim's wild turkey, squirrel
meat, and oyster dressing.

Always the click of the mantel clock
and hourly chime, a different time
than twelve miles up the road
toward Springfield, toward home—

Pop-Tarts in the toaster;
Tang, like the astronauts;
Chef Boyardee in a box.

UPON HEARING JAMES STILL READ
*"THOSE I WANT IN HEAVEN WITH ME
SHOULD THERE BE SUCH A PLACE"*
Hindman Settlement School, Hindman, Kentucky

Late July evening,
half moon over mountain trees,
crickets swoon in the near grass.
Voices, shafts of warm light,
flow from the crowded hall.
Awed faces halo around him.

I had never met the man, too young
to have read much he'd written, yet
I am weeping—
his husky likeness to my grandfather,
black eyeglass case
comfortable in the pocket
over his heart—
for their generation gone.

Mr. Still, should there be such a place
as heaven, when you go there,
look him up.
What stories you could share—
your dog, Jack, curled at your feet,
his hound, Pixie, dreaming rabbits
beside him, and all those true
characters gathered 'round.

Be with them there.

ALLAN

He explodes from the classroom into the student
chair set in the hallway for this purpose.
"Bad day, Allan?" I ask.
My hand touches his close-cropped hair.
"Yes." He shudders. "They're all bad."
The teacher screams a last harassment.

His head seems too heavy for his neck
and shoulders to sustain. He slumps,
then surfaces again. I offer a smile,
but it is nothing.

I see the shape of his life already.
His small body bent in waves, he struggles
to float, fighting the current. Finally, he tires.
The need for silence pulls him down.

All he's ever wanted
is to be left
alone.

THE SLOWEST BOY IN THE WORLD

walks four, maybe five, no six steps
behind the other children.
He starts near the front of the line,
 his teacher knows his habits
but then a bump on the wall, so small
no one else sees it, calls to him
 it could be an ant or unusual beetle
and he must reach out
to touch its brown smudgy wonder.
By then the whole rascally crew has pushed
past him, their shirts spotted and damp
from drinking fountain trickery.

At recess, while the other children swing madly
to and fro, half-laced sneakers pumping skyward
the slowest boy in the world watches workers sawing bricks
 electric noise! dust clouds! white-masked faces!
as a window shape takes form. No glass, not yet,
but he can imagine the clear pane, men straining
to lift the magnificent rectangle.

Already he's used to being different, has learned
to ignore the names and scolding
 hurry up slow poke! you'll never get there that way!
and a few understand, save him the last cookie
or a piece of blue construction paper.
Each day amazes, magnifies, maddens
 must he write the alphabet again? who cares
  what the stupid giraffe said to the elephant?
but what glory lunch brings—
piling peas carefully between chicken nuggets,
the untapped intricacies of gravy and rolls.

ALL THE LITTLE SCHOOLS

Tonight in the village of Rutland, cars and pick-up trucks
fill the school lot and side streets. Gymnasium doors
open to warm light reflecting off waxed wooden floors.
Parents, teachers, children wander in and out of
bright rooms for the last Open House.
Chimney swifts circle above.

Down the road, closer to the county seat, bulldozers
razed hills and trees, a century house, for a new school
underway. All the little schools—
Salisbury, Bradbury, Harrisonville, Salem Center—
turn ghostly. Soon Rutland too will close.

Families gather under first stars, the sky lingering
purple and gray. On the playground, a few kids swing high,
old chain links squeaking as they rise then dip low, but it is
the swifts that draw eyes upward, the air alive with their
chatter as they loop then dive for home.

The birds swirl closer and closer as if caught in a whirlpool
they can't control, then in a flash they are gone, down
the chimney, all except one.
Finally, finally, he goes.

Parents turn then, call to their children. There is still
homework to be done. Lights blaze briefly
as families tumble into cars and trucks.
The old school slips into darkness,
chimney swifts fluttering
like a heart.

THROWING STONES

Standing on a back-road bridge, I throw
stones into burnished water. Below
a catfish appears brown as summer tea,
shadow in a shadow pool, a shimmering
spatula spreading muddy icing.
This stream was declared dead months ago, yet
she is here, and others come soft-footed from the woods.

Soon roiling orange water, poisoned deep in black tunnels
will swell over these familiar stones. Already pumps begin.
Men digging coal, burning money, have signed this death
to stall their own, a future they cannot fix with chemical
cleansers, silent water foaming at the shore.
This time, not one will get away.

FOSSIL FUELED

Along the ancient river elements collide.
Mammoth humps of coal
coil like black-spined dinosaurs.
Squat volcanoes spew sulfurous air.
Above skeletal limbs of steel
unnatural clouds accumulate—
cumulous, ponderous swamps of sky,
absurd meteorological masses.

Long jagged claws scalp green hills,
scrape out the innards of abundant mountains—
the mother regurgitates her blackened core
to feed our endless hunger.
We hide subdued, obedient,
wired in our sun-bright caves
fearing sudden darkness more
than a distant grave.

A LONGING LIKE NOAH'S

Three days and nights the rains have come,
not yet Old Testament, but long enough.
Adrift on our hill in the gloom of trees,
we have no place to go, no road we can see.

Below in the valley flood torments,
villages and farm fields overflow.
Houses gape, vacant as couches
floating down Main Street.

Loss everywhere, heavy as stone.

DRINKING TEA AT A MCDONALD'S OVERLOOKING THE OHIO RIVER AT POMEROY, OHIO

Surrounded by plastic and paper wrappers,
I hug Styrofoam, scoop spilled sugar
into crystal peaks. Alone, by the window
I read James Wright, his *wasted life*
hammock-bound in Pine Island, Minnesota.
Outside rain slices the sky,
the swollen Ohio lifts the debris of storms.
Suddenly, I am grateful to be where I am,
awash in fluorescence, waist-deep
in man-made delight.

A NORMAL DAY
"Thank God for a normal day."
—sign in front of an Episcopal Church
after severe flooding along the Ohio River

Creeping truck and hose the length of the waterfront
a fireman power washes mud off the walking path.
Shopkeepers cart and carry soggy remnants of their wares
to dumpsters hulking at the curb. The Court House remains
dark, cases continued, streets beribboned with caution tape
as if a crime has occurred. Tree limbs and hay bales
park in the riverside lot instead of cars, and gazebo benches
drift toward Cincinnati like phantoms in the current.

But the sun is shining and the angry river's slowed its pace.
Barges heavy with coal and oil, once again, churn muddy waters.
Families muck out houses, almost cheerful after wading through
hip-boot days of rain. Children board each yellow bus bursting
with bravado comparing flood tales with friends. On the radio,
local banks and car lots advertise hope: 0% financing
for qualifying customers, FEMA's on the way, and the
Sternwheeler Festival has been rescheduled
for this weekend.

Everything's going to be okay.

PASSING POEMS

All morning the science teacher collected notes
passed clandestinely, hand to hand, folded like
intricate flowers. She opened them prepared
for scandal—
Did you kiss Justin? Check one___yes___no
Instead she pounced on poems.

She storms into the English room
while students are at band or choir
demanding an explanation. She's
suspicious—the writing's rather good.
She's unused to academic passion.

Guilty party, visiting writer, I raise
my hand, thrust back into the third
seat, second row of adolescence where
survival of the fittest was a daily show.
I read them Whitman, I whisper.

She stares at me as if I've stashed
marijuana under my chair or crammed
a locker with bottles of Scotch, luring
innocents into dangerous land.

But I smile, knowing I've already got them.
They're bitten. Poetry's quick venom plows
through their veins, oozing their angst,
their pain. I've started something.
I hope it spreads.

THE ROAD MARKED POETRY

Directions to the poetry festival seem purposefully
vague as if the founders invited the famous poets
to read just for them, then told the rest of us as an
afterthought. Yet, my friend and I are persistent.
Though GPS fails us, we turn down the road marked
Poetry, the hand-scrawled sign so juvenile it can only
have been made by a child in disguise.

A mile or so through the woods, a hint of lake appears
and a white-framed shed on a newly green field
with cars scattered nearby, but no sign saying you
have arrived safely, or at all. Unsure, we drive on.
If we don't see another sign, we say, we will turn
around, go back, and park in the unmarked field
and enter the unmarked door.

Soon the road narrows with houses sitting tight
on the lakeshore. We sail past to the end where road
becomes muddy trail, then back through the fairy tale
village—slow, slower, slower—as a peacock steps out
like a king from the shadows. We stop, roll down
the window, and a boy, brown face lit by smiles,
answers before we ask the question.

"No, no, he's not mine. He belongs to the neighbor."
With a laugh, he shoos the iridescent bird out of the road.
We cruise the hill again, park the car, moving our bodies
toward music. Cautiously, we push open the scuffed white
door and enter an unfamiliar room full of unfamiliar
people, but we have come this far. Surely
Poetry has found us.

APPALACHIAN WINE

The sun slips down
    into the green easiness
        of hills

In the pond
    a bullfrog draws
        deep drafts of dusk

Above the barn
    one golden maple
        gleams like a goblet

Night's cork
    shudders loose
        pours a burgundy sky

WALNUTS

For days the woods have spit them down,
the ground littered and rolling with rough
green pods. Walnuts ricochet
off the barn's tin roof or grumble
thunder, no rain in sight.

The water trough stained brown and bobbing,
wild beasts skitter with each new breeze.
Autumn's air raid thumps a warning:
winter is coming, keep
moving, save.

WRITING THE STORM

All morning I wait—
bare trees, bare page.

I long for those first
white flakes, swirling black
words to settle around me.

The sky broods; I brood too.
Then, without warning,
a sudden squall—

snow piles up, tracks
appear on the page.

Later, the sun
revises.

DRIVEN

Lady beetles range over sun-warmed glass
like rusty Volkswagens spotted by age.
They zoom in exodus from fluorescent cities
searching for exits, wings unfurled.

Stuck in February, we rise with them, press
faces to windows toward the open road.
Spring hums within us, to fly, to woo.
We unfold new maps. Set a course for June.

WEATHER REPORT

Winter did not come this year.
Even the groundhog declared this one a bust.
Rain fell; random ice felled us.
Day after day, we sloshed through mud,
hating the same clouds. The thermometer
hung in boredom drifting only briefly
from its middling plumb.

This morning, finches and titmice
peddle vigorous songs, too busy
to perch at our feeders full of longing
and cracked corn. The deer also
stay away, woodland browsing
plentiful and far.

Only we miss snow days deep
with stories—our last excuse
for discovering fire.

WHEN WISHES WERE HORSES

They are out again—
one a ragged roan pony
prone to kicking the dogs, chasing the cat,
nipping would-be riders retreating
to safer ground; the other, a paint that
heels like a mutt and comes halfway
through the kitchen door nosing for carrots.

Fearful of barbed wire, the crack and sizzle
of an electric charge, we who knew horses
from John Wayne, Roy Rogers, and glossy
calendars, strung high-tensile wire, imagining
groomed, glistening guests content with hay
and their contained green.

Now in a downpour, the ponies nose out, step
gracefully between bottom and middle wires,
nuzzling tender grass in the yard. I approach
hiding lead ropes behind me, offering apples
as I go. They stare with wild brown eyes,
forelegs poised to bolt. Rain rolls off all of us.

Inside the fence, the mustang watches,
mouth carefully working the hay. He could
easily jump the fence, or force it down, yet
he, of all, seems content and ponders these
innovators with horse disdain—
they who have known only barn and paddock,
sweet crunchy oats and elegant hay.

Escapees from heaven.

HEAVENLY

For two hours I dig in November light,
peeling off sweaters and gloves
as the sun glides higher—
twenty-seven Triumph tulips, fifteen
Salome daffodils, snowdrops, Miss Vain
crocus, twenty allium in the ground.

All the roses pruned and put to bed,
yarrow trimmed, the Rose of Sharon
contained once more.

The fat black cat and his butterscotch
sister roll drunk in catnip. One redbird,
countless nuthatches and chickadees
chatter for seed.

Inside the house, I scrub brown earth
from under my nails, choose
a golden apple to eat.
With shaking arms, I pour
a tall glass of chocolate milk
and drink.

GETTING THE MAIL

Paper is the heart of it—
words coming and going, the mystery
of what's hinged behind that door—
but this is only part of it.
I walk down the long driveway of stones,
glossy tulip poplar leaves tumble at my feet.
Cats slip from barns purring rings
around my ankles. My dog and the neighbor's
dogs bay and tremble with each new scent, and
the road lies open, twisting questions
just out of sight.
News rises over mountains spreading
wings from an envelope of flame, a red-
tailed hawk spins circles above me, calling,
crying my name.

Cathy Cultice Lentes is a poet, essayist, and children's writer. She has been writing and publishing since the age of eight when her first poem appeared in a small-town Ohio newspaper. She was born in Xenia and grew up near Springfield. Since 1987, she has lived and worked in the Appalachian foothills of southeast Ohio, a few winding miles from the Ohio River, halfway between Cincinnati and Pittsburgh.

Lentes' work appears in various literary journals, magazines, and anthologies including *Every River on Earth: Writing from Appalachian Ohio* (Ohio University Press, 2015) and *Quarried: Three Decades of Pine Mountain Sand & Gravel* (Dos Madres Press, 2015). She is the recipient of the Judson Jerome Scholarship in Poetry, a residency at The Vermont Studio Center, and was the winner of a 2014 Work-in-Progress Grant from the Society of Children's Book Writers and Illustrators. Lentes served as a juror for the 2015-2016 reading series of the Women of Appalachia—Women Speak Project and has been a longtime participant. She shares her love of books and writing with students from kindergarten-age to adult. In 2003, community and state officials recognized her as a Woman Making a Difference in the Arts.

Lentes is a 2013 graduate of the Solstice MFA Program of Pine Manor College. Find out more about her life and work at www.cathyculticelentes.com.

CPSIA information can be obtained at www.ICGtesting.com
Printed in the USA
BVOW08s1354060716

454556BV00002B/8/P